SHINE BOY

SHINE BOY

stories and photographs by José Galvez

with Annie Galvez

For information and permissions, contact
Shine Boy Media, LLC
PO Box 52575
Durham, NC 27717

Designed by Annie Galvez

First edition: September 2009

ISBN: 978-0-9824339-0-4

Printed in the United States of America
by School of the Graphic Arts, Masonic Home for Children, Oxford, North Carolina.

10 9 8 7 6 5 4 3 2 1

Photo caption, page ii: SHOESHINE BOYS∗TUCSON, AZ∗1973

Contents

Prologue vii

Sailing in the Desert 15

The Marble King 21

The Picnic 27

Picking Cotton 33

Going to Nana's 41

Shining Shoes 49

Ronquillo's Bakery 55

Selling Papers 61

Christmas 71

Barber Shop 77

Entering the Newsroom 85

About José 93

CHILDREN ON THE FRONT STOOP∗TUCSON,AZ∗1978

Prologue

For forty years I've photographed Latinos in the United States. Countless times, I've had a viewer grab me by the arm, pull me over to a photograph in an exhibit or book, and say, "that looks just like my" tía, cousin, grandfather.

Other times I've had people launch into stories from their lives, inspired by my work. My photograph may be from a very different time or very different place, but it somehow strikes a note in the souls of the people looking at it, and I'm the lucky recipient of a piece of their history.

I am telling my own history in the photographs. As I walk around Latino communities with my camera, I am connected to the people I see. I recognize them as family. Inklings, memories rise within me. I am inspired to raise the camera and immortalize the moment.

Those little boys hanging out in Los Angeles remind me of myself when I ran around the streets, working and getting into trouble, sometimes both. Those girls putting on makeup remind me of my tías and my mother getting ready to go to the Saturday night dances. That teenager just new from Mexico who is working construction is not so far removed from my father and his brothers who built my abuelos' house. This elderly woman has that gleaming, no-nonsense eye and strong hands like my Nana.

This book is comprised of some of my childhood memories set beside photographs I've taken throughout my career. The pictures are like details in my life story and reveal how my memories continue to shape my work.

As a group, the stories give you a glimpse into what it was like for a poor Mexican boy like me to grow up in the 1950s in Tucson, Arizona. It was a time when I could walk around downtown in the evening hours by myself, watched after by adults who asked my name and took me under their wing. It was a time when a marble tournament was a big event and when a dollar made a difference in what we ate that week.

COUPLE RESTING IN SHADE ✳ DURHAM, NC ✳ 2008

The stories may be limited by my
childhood perspective. The people
in them may remember things differ-
ently and I hope they forgive me if the
stories seem incomplete. They are true
to what I knew and how I felt.

As in many Mexican and Mexican-
American families, we had nick-
names. I use them here in the stories.
We always called my brother Jay,
"Chem" short for "Chemale." My
cousin William Galvez, we called
"Güero." I was "Galvitos" or "Joe."
When we come together to celebrate
a wedding or mourn at a funeral, we
still call each other by these names.
They bind us together. Later, when I

was active in the Chicano Movement, I reclaimed "José," rejecting the Anglicization of my name for all but my closest family.

I am so grateful for this life I've led. I thank my brothers, Jay and Bob. They are kind-hearted, smart, funny men and I'm lucky to have shared these adventures with them. Both of them are also much better cooks than I am. My sister Sylvia was a great woman. She died a few years ago from diabetes complications and we miss her.

Life wouldn't have been the same for me if I hadn't loved Chata from the beginning. My best cousin, known as Mercedes Gastelum to the rest of the world, has supported me and believed in me. She would do anything for me. Don't mess with me or you'll have her to deal with.

My mother Lupe was the biggest influence in my life. She gave me my independence. She had only a second grade education and had spent her young life caring for her father before becoming our mother. She suffered from epilepsy and arthritis, but did what she could. She wasn't always sure why I needed to succeed. She was taught in the Mexican way that being *ambioso* was bad. But when I look back on it, she only half-heartedly tried to keep me from my studies. I think she was proud of me.

My father José was a good man. He was rarely at home. He worked out of town a lot as a farm worker, a miner, and a lumberjack. Also, he had his demons, things a child doesn't really know about, and he often lived down the block with his brother or a friend. I do remember the good times when he was with us. When he came home from work, he had always saved part of his lunch and I couldn't wait until he opened his bucket to reveal the surprise apple or half a cookie he'd kept just for me.

I was twelve when my dad died, but even before that men entered my life and showed me what it meant to be strong and brave and honest. I carry their lessons with me because whether they intended it or not, they filled a hole in my life. They guided me and led me. They watched out for me and taught me. They were very present father figures.

Charlie Soto not only got me my first job at the newspaper but he also dealt strongly with me when he later caught me stealing. He gave me one fateful choice and I thank him for setting me straight. Buster Durazo and Rudy Padias not only let me hang out with them, they also fed me and kept me busy. They taught me the value of working for yourself and making your own way.

All those men from the newsroom were more than role models. I would never have gone on to be a photojournalist, I would never have covered presidents, and I would never have won a Pulitzer Prize if not for their steady guidance when I was a teenager.

These stories end with my walking into the newsroom but you should know that after that day, Ed Gallardo, Jack Sheaffer, Vic Thornton, Harry Goldstein, Don Carson, and all the other editors, reporters, and photographers at the *Arizona Daily Star* set me on a career path that has brought me incredible joy and fulfillment ever since.

They made a way for me to go to camp in the summers. They made a way for me to work as a copy boy, making money but also getting my homework done. They made a way for me to be the first one in my family to graduate from college.

Now that's inspiring. ✳

GIRLS PLAYING IN PUDDLE*TUCSON, AZ*1972

Sailing in the Desert

for Chata, my favorite

The monsoons were coming. My cousin Chata and I looked over the fence and up into the sky at the dark, heavy clouds rising in the south. Soon they would march their way across the city, leaving in their wake enormous puddles and flooded streets.

Tata was sitting on his rocker on our small front porch. Nana was nearby tending her roses. The pink flowers were drooping in the heat. On the grapevines small clusters of baby grapes were covered with bags so the birds wouldn't eat them.

Chata lived in the big house. My mom, siblings, and I lived with my abuelos in a small two-room *casita* beside it. We went inside the big house to eat lunch. Tía Mercy had made burritos filled with scrambled eggs and beans. She had used Nana's homemade tortillas. We ate as many as we could. I made a milk mustache.

15

Dink…dink…dink. Just then, the first fat drops hit the tin roof. We ran to the window and watched the rain begin to pour. It sounded like a never-ending string of firecrackers.

Lightning slashed across the sky and Chata and I jumped. The thunder that followed it shook the house. Little by little, the street outside turned into a river.

Mom came running into the house. She held a dishtowel over her head and her ankles were soaked.

"Can we go out now?" I pleaded.

"Not yet. You better wait," said Mom.

It hadn't rained like this since I could remember. But then I was only five.

Nothing could tear Chata and me from that window. We stood there for most of the afternoon while the storm raged. This was better than television. Long gray branches torn from the eucalyptus tree next door floated by. A cardboard box went sailing slowly and then got

CHATA AND VANESSA✳TUCSON, AZ✳1996

caught in an eddy and crumpled. The deep green smell of wet creosote snuck under the sash.

After it stopped thundering, people emerged to stand on their porches and look up at the sky. Mr. Avalos came home from work in his railroad overalls, pushing his shins through the water that was knee-deep in spots. A car passed carefully. Its driver had both hands on the wheel.

Mom and my tía were having another cup of coffee at the kitchen table. They waved their hands toward the door when they saw us, laughing. "¡Sí, sí, ándenles!" We didn't even need to ask. We ran outside.

"Let's build a boat," I said to Chata.

Neither of us desert kids had ever seen a real boat.

"There's a pile of wood over by the shed," Chata said.

We ran barefoot over the muddy yard, making sure to step in all the little lakes, trying to splash each other as we went. We searched through the pile. I held up a big plank just big enough for one of us to sit on.

We dragged it out to the street.

We waded out and set the plank in the water which was moving swiftly. We took turns pretending we were floating on a wild river. I found a tree branch and was soon reeling in the biggest fish ever seen in the barrio. Chata snarled like a pirate and commanded me to give up my gold.

My skin was still damp when I went to bed that night. I dreamed of whales and buried treasure. *

PLAYING IN THE STREETS * TUCSON, AZ * 1977

The Marble King

Our yard was dominated by a large mulberry tree that dropped its black sticky fruit all over the place in summer. Nana's garden occupied the back corner, open to the sun. The rest of the yard was mostly dirt.

It wasn't much space to play in and all the games we had fit into our hands. We played jacks. We jumped rope. And we loved hide and seek.

I can't remember when I learned to play marbles but I'm sure it was my cousin Güero who taught me. He was older and bigger than all of us, with broad shoulders and strong arms. Later, he would become a great high school football player, beloved by the city.

In our eyes, Güero was already an established pro marble shooter. He kept his prize marbles in a drawstring bag. If you dared to challenge him, you were going to lose.

He would kneel down in the dirt and draw a circle with his stout finger. Only then would he open his bag and slowly take out his marbles one by one like jewels. Our eyes were large at the Cat's Eyes and Peewees. He had agates and big Old Bowlers and Steelies. They were of all different colors and as well, of all different sizes.

The rules were simple. It was one against one. Each player would put five marbles into the circle. Then with your best shooters, you would shoot them into the ring, trying to knock your opponent's marbles outside the circle.

There were many different ways to shoot marbles. You could loft it into the air with your thumb, letting it bounce strategically. You could knuckle down, resting your knuckles on the ground and thumbing the marble sideways. You could hold it with the index finger for more aim or the middle finger if you needed speed, flicking it with your other hand.

We played for keeps. Any marbles you knocked out were yours. And when you played against Güero, he went home with a heavier bag. As the games raged and we lost them all, we begged each other for loaners to keep playing.

KIDS' TRACK MEET∗TUCSON, AZ∗1979

One day Güero invited us to come watch him shoot marbles in a city-wide competition in the park. We were very excited. We'd never seen anything like it. Children would come from all over town to compete. And we were sure that Güero would win.

The whole family was there to see it. Güero's parents and siblings already made a large cheering section. Then we arrived and Chata, Eddie, Junior, Bob and I elbowed each other for a better view. Around us different contests were going on. Each circle had two players and as the contests were decided, the winners moved on to challenge other winners.

Güero was advancing. He took the contest seriously. It was like watching a golfer line up a putt or a pool player, a shot. Güero would pace around the ring, assessing the terrain, looking for vulnerable marbles and choosing his line of attack.

And then there were two. Güero had made it to the final round against a boy none of us knew. We held our breath as Güero found his target and dubbed nearly half his opponent's marbles in the first shot. The other boy never had a chance.

Güero had won. Later, he strutted around with his enormous trophy. It was over a foot tall and on top had a shiny, gold boy thumbing a marble. We gathered around it and its winner.

Güero was now more of a champ than ever. After that, we all tried harder at our backyard tournaments, hoping that maybe someday we too would get good enough to bring home a trophy. ✳

TETHERBALL ON A STREET SIGN✳LOS ANGELES, CA✳1983

FAMILY PICNIC ON MT. LEMMON*TUCSON, AZ*1999

The Picnic

for Jay

I could smell the tortillas frying on the stove. I could hear my mother and
father and aunt and uncle coming in and out of the house, banging the
drawers in the kitchen, opening and shutting the refrigerator. I jumped a
little at the thump of something heavy on the porch.

Sleepy-eyed but curious, I emerged from the bed. Nana was at the stove.
Tía Mercy was busy mixing macaroni salad. Tío Avalino was just outside
the door, filling the metal ice chest with chicken, *carne*, and soda pops.

Chata sat at the table with a hot tortilla in her hands. "We're going on a
picky-nicky," she said, "to Patagonia!"

Patagonia sounded like a magical place on the other side of the world. I
had never been out of the city before so I couldn't imagine what it looked
like.

Dad's red pickup was sitting in front of the house. Mom and my baby sister Sylvia were already sitting in the cab. We boys got in the back wedging ourselves between a load of firewood, a pile of blankets, and a hard ice chest. In the backseat of my tío's car, I could see Tía Mercy's arm around Chata's moving, talking head. Nana and Tata sat patiently in front, eyes forward. Tío jerked his thumb at my father and shut the door. We were off.

My brothers and I sat as tall as we could as we wound our way through the barrio. We waved and shouted to people on the sidewalk, excited to share news of our adventure. Soon, nothing looked familiar. The houses were fewer and farther apart. Then all we could see was desert.

We nestled down in the truck and watched as the city disappeared on the horizon. All around us were miles of cactus. The pickup began to labor as we started to climb. The cactus turned to scrub with grass in between. We went up and down hills. Chem spotted a herd of cattle and we all scrambled to the side to look.

Then there were trees all around and we went deeper into the woods. When the pickup finally stopped, we jumped out into cooler air that smelled of green. There was a creek with running water.

Bobby and I saw the swing at the same time. A rope dangled from a tall tree. We took turns running toward it with all our strength and flying high out over the water. All day long we played. Chem and I threw rocks. Chata and I tried to catch frogs. We went swimming, splashing each other.

Along the grassy bank, Nana wandered. She had taken off her shoes and walked carefully over the rocks. She was gathering leafy plants and putting them in her dress. Tata sat, like he always did, watching us without smiling. In the clearing, Mom and Tía were at a wooden table, fussing and chatting as they put out the food. My father and Tío were laughing by a small fire.

The smell of the mesquite smoke came drifting over to us. I imagined myself a cowboy out on the range with my herd of cattle. We had stopped at a pond to water the horses.

We came out of the water dripping and Tía
Mercy gathered us together. "We're going
hunting," she said. We all bit our lips with
anticipation.

"For dinner?" asked Bobby, giggling.

"For *bellotas*," she said, drawing out the last
word.

She showed us the trees and pointed out
the small brown nuts that littered the
ground. I picked one up and looked at
it closely. It was smooth like it had been
tumbled by the river. On its top was a small
cap. I couldn't believe that the huge ram-
bling tree in front of me came out of this
tiny little acorn.

30

Tía Mercy bit into one with her front teeth and then pulled it apart for us to see. Inside, the nut was white and flaky. She offered it to me for a taste. It was sweet and delicious, but barely a mouthful. She left us to our hunt and we competed to see who could find the biggest one. We threw as many at each other as we ate.

"Come and get it!" came a yell. We dropped the nuts and ran.

The table was so full we could barely find room for our plates. There was a pile of roast chicken and carne. There was green chile salsa and orange sodas. Nana had put the plants she had gathered into the beans and added chopped onion. We ate until we could barely move.

Evening was coming and the fire had died down. It was time to go.

There was enough room in the bed of the truck now for us to lie down. I watched as the mesmerizing stars flew by overhead. They were closer out here than in the city. By the time I woke up I was home. ✷

FARMWORKER ON BUS*CALEXICO, CA*1985

Picking Cotton

for Bob, my partner in crime

"It's too early," I protested, squirming deeper into the bed.

"*Andalé, José!* You said you wanted to go to work with me. We have to get there early or we'll miss the bus," replied my father. "Besides, your brother is already up and dressed."

Bob was always trying to beat me at everything.

Dad had made a few burritos and I ate quickly while he sipped his coffee. We snuck quietly out of the house and into the dark. I could see the shadows of the downtown buildings that loomed before us. There were no lights on in any of the houses we passed.

I was certain that we were absolutely alone and that everybody else was still sleeping. But then we got to the stop and saw a group of men and boys there, standing silently, rubbing their hands to keep warm in the crisp, desert air. Bobby and I stuck close together. The other boys looked at us through sleepy eyes. We sized them up and knew we were the youngest.

I had been on a bus only once when we had gone to Nana's house for her birthday. We had stood in our best clothes by the road under a sign and a big city bus had stopped with a whoosh of air. Its door opened out. Chem, the oldest, took the coins from where he had been protecting them, and paid for all of us. We filed into the bus behind him, my mother pushing us from behind. Chem chose a seat and Mom sat with him, holding Sylvia. Bob and I sat across from them, fighting for the window.

It was exciting riding the bus that day, watching the city go by. I liked the loud sound of the brakes as the bus stopped over and over. Sometimes we stopped fast and leaned forward, clutching the back of the seat. Other times the bus driver slid the big vehicle smoothly up to the curb. The bell rang above my head as people tottered toward the front. I liked watching the people get on and off. There were women with shopping bags and men going to work.

But this was a different kind of bus. Once we got on, there was no stopping. The streetlights twinkled by and then we were out in the indigo country where there were no lights. The sky began to lighten and I could see wide fields come into focus. When the bus finally stopped, the sun had dawned from behind the mountains casting long rays across the flat land.

There were rows and rows of plants with little tuffs of white poking out from them. *Algodón.* Cotton.

We got off the bus and filed over to the back of a truck. There were men in charge who handed each of us a long, gray sack with a strap. Mimicking our father, Bob and I hoisted the bags over our shoulders.

Dad taught us how to reach into the plant. We were to pull the fluff from the middle of the cotton bolls with our fingers and put it in our sack. We were not to miss any. He pointed to an open row. Bob and I worked in the same aisle. I picked the plants to the left and Bobby, the ones to the right.

SHINE BOY

HEADED TO THE FIELDS∗IMPERIAL VALLEY, CA∗1985

"I don't think it's ever going to get full," I muttered to my brother. It seemed like we had been stuffing our bags forever and we had barely moved a few feet. Now I knew why Dad had us wear long sleeve shirts and straw hats. By now the sun was up above us, making us squint, and the plants caught on our hands, drying our skin and making it itch.

"I'm thirsty." "When are going to eat?" Bob and I worked steadily but kept up our complaints. I stood up from my hunched position and looked around. All across the field, the hats of men and boys bent and rose. I couldn't see anyone's face and tried to find my father by looking for his long, thin back.

When I went back to work, the bag sagged heavy on my shoulder. We were making progress. Soon, we had reached the end of our row.

"What do we do now?" asked Bob.

"Hey, you two, are you ready for some lunch?" yelled Dad from a distance. He came toward us carrying a bulging bag in his left hand. He had been up and down several rows in the time it took us to do one.

We followed him back to the truck and had our bags weighed by the men and the amount written down next to our names. I had never been so hungry and the cold burritos Dad had packed were delicious. Bob and I drank long from the thermos. We sat with other workers in the shade of a lone tree. No one spoke much.

"Okay guys, back to work," said Dad.

On the way home, Bob was leaning against the window, asleep. I laid my small, aching hand on the brown, strong hand of my father as the bus rumbled into the growing dusk.

He smiled. "I bet you'll never want to come out here with me again."

But we did. It was one of the few times we had gotten to spend the whole day with him. ✳

SLEEPING IN THE ONION FIELD✳EL MIRAGE, AZ✳1985

BOY BETWEEN ABUELAS∗TUCSON, AZ∗1971

Going to Nana's

It was a hot Sunday afternoon. I had returned from selling my papers outside the cathedral. Bob and I had had our lunch. We now sat on the stoop. We watched a lizard scurry across the wall. We gave up on finding good music on the radio.

"Let's go see Nana," I said.

Years earlier, we had left our abuelos behind and had moved into government housing. Visiting Nana became one of our favorite weekend activities.

Bobby tied up his shoelaces and we ventured into the neighborhood. We ran our hands along the fences and across the long stuccoed walls of the adobes that rose directly from the sidewalk. Down the street, a neighbor sat on her stoop. She waved wearily.

I don't remember Bob and me ever talking about our route. Yet over all the years we wandered to Nana's, we always took the same path and made the same stops.

First we walked by El Tiradito, where the strong adobe wall protected the candles and dying flowers left by unseen visitors. We kicked the dirt wondering if the legend was true. Did a man really die for love so long ago and was he buried somewhere under our feet? Bob and I looked for evidence until the thought of ghosts made us run.

We went next to Moreno's butcher shop. The screen door banged behind us. The counter seemed to stretch for miles. We peered into the cases and saw ground meats and whole chickens, tongues and *tripas*. On the other wall was another counter. There were enormous pickles floating in a jar. Another held pig's feet. Another, boiled eggs. Another, *saladitos*. Just looking at the salty prunes made my cheeks water.

There was also candy. We looked at the colorful jawbreakers and the bubble gums of all flavors. We pulled the change out of our pockets and rolled it in our hands, trying to decide. Finally we bought a grape soda and two candy bars, and unwrapped them as we headed back onto the bright sidewalk.

The parking lot of the Latin Social Club was a mess. Long streamers clung to rocks and rose occasionally in the light breeze. A man swept with a huge broom, leaning his shoulders into the work.

"Looks like they had a dance last night." We watched the man for a while and munched our candy.

On the edge of downtown, we lingered at the junkyard. There were new wrecks to see. Once in a while, we'd be lucky and we'd actually see a tow truck pull up with another mangled car. We pointed out the worst ones to each other and wondered what had happened and whom it had happened to. Every now and then we snuck onto the lot and would search the cars for loose coins on the floor and anything else that was left behind.

Beyond this, the sidewalk dipped downhill and we entered another world, Snob Hollow. Here large houses sat back from the street. There were shrubs and grass, gates and gardens. We would hang by our hands, our heads peeking up through the wrought iron, marveling. We would run our hands on the cool stone walls.

Some of the houses even had second floors. I'd been in only one place that had a second floor: school. But not a house. I'd never been in a house that wasn't squat low to the ground. In Snob Hollow, the lofty eucalyptus trees swayed and the houses too stood tall.

I took off. "Let's go see what's in the wash." At the end of summer, the wash could have water in it, brought there by the monsoon rains. Today we found tiny guppies to hold in our hands and inspect. Bob hopped after a small frog, trying not to get his shoes wet.

The wash snuck through a tunnel passing under the road on its way to the Santa Cruz River a few blocks away. We dared each other to go as far into the tunnel as possible. The farther I went in, the deeper the darkness became. The water held unseen creatures at my feet. I walked slower and slower, my hands against the tunnel walls. The gloom was thick and spooky. I screamed and spun, running back to the light. Bobby laughed loud at me and called me a scaredy cat.

We hiked to the top of a big mound of earth. Below, the freeway was being built to take traffic around the city rather than through it. Each time, we looked off toward the north, hands over our eyes, to see how far it stretched. Everyone knew it came straight from Phoenix,

BOYS CARRYING BOTTLES ∗ TUCSON, AZ ∗ 1969

twisting around long, flats of desert, but we'd never been.

In front of us lay Barrio Hollywood, our old neighborhood. From this height we could see the large tamarisk trees that lined the river bank and the old brick yard beyond it. Way in the distance on the edge of the barrio rose St. Mary's Hospital where we were born.

We poked around the construction, crossing the carved-out and dusty roadbed that would soon be paved. Earth-moving machines sat silent, waiting for the men to return.

And then the *cimarrona* stand called. The man in the stand scooped crushed ice into pointed paper cups and then gave us our choice of the many colored liquids. I always picked root beer, and he squeezed the brown syrup over my cup till the ice grew thick and heavy and melted a little in my hand.

These we licked and munched the last few blocks to Nana's house. Tata was gone now, but she still lived in the small *casita* where we spent our youngest days. It was painted green and had a small ramada in front where she would sit and clean beans for the pot.

Nana never knew we were coming but every time we arrived, she tucked us under her arms and brought us into the cool house.

"Vengan, M'ijos. Comemos," she'd always say. She knew that was one reason we came. From her garden, she'd pull fresh vegetables and make *calabacitas, frijoles, arroz.* Around these we'd wrap her warm handmade tortillas.

We'd leave, filled and happy, running back so we could get home before sundown. ✳

WOMAN IN DOORWAY∗TUCSON,AZ∗1978

SHINE BOY

BOY ON BICYCLE∗TUCSON, AZ∗1979

Shining Shoes

That morning, Dad sent me to Jerry Lee Ho's grocery store for some wood. I poked around the back door where the produce stackers had tossed crates and boxes. There were bits of discarded fruit and vegetables everywhere, filling the air with a heavy smell. I found two crates, one a little smashed, and carried them home to my father.

My father could build anything. When I was smaller, I watched as he and his brothers built a house together. Now he was building me my future.

He showed me how to pull the crates apart with the claw of a hammer. Then he sawed the pieces to just the right length. He took nails from his pocket and fashioned a box. He put a small piece across the top.

"To keep your customers' shoes from slipping," he said. Then he rubbed the wood smooth with a piece of sandpaper.

Dad had finally made me a shoeshine box. I had been pestering him for weeks. Other boys were running around downtown shining shoes and getting paid for it. Mike Tatum told me that he made about a dollar a day, and even more on Saturdays when he could work all day.

I imagined all the things I could do with my very own dollar. The movies cost a quarter, a cimarrona cost a nickel, and a meal at Jake's Chili Dogs cost forty cents. I was excited.

"Now we need to get your supplies," he said holding out two dollar bills. "You can pay me back with your earnings."

Dad and I went that afternoon to the shoe store and bought two brushes, two shine rags, a round tin of saddle soap, a small towel, a small brush, and black and brown polish.

"I see that you're ready to start your new career as a shoeshine boy," Mom remarked after we had returned and I was placing my supplies in the box. She stood over me smiling.

"There's one more thing you have to do before I let you out the door. When you get home each day, you will share half of your earnings with me. Do we have a deal?"

DANCING COUPLE∗TUCSON, AZ∗1999

"I guess so," I meekly replied.

I already owed my father two dollars.
Now I was going to hand more money
over to my mother. Still, I agreed to it all.
Off I ran, my shoeshine box under my
arm, to downtown to try my luck.

I had watched the other boys closely and
knew exactly what to do. When I saw
a man coming my way, I stood up tall
and looked him right in the eye. "Shine,
Mister?" I asked.

If he said yes, the man would lean
against the wall and put his foot up on
my box. I would whip out my brush and
remove any mud or dust. Then I would

load up my small brush with saddle soap and cover the shoe with it, being careful not to get it on the man's socks. The soap was creamy and thick and it drew the dirt out of a shoe's seams. I would wipe that off and pull out my tin of shoe polish. Taking a dab with my brush, I'd rub that into the shoe.

Then came the big finish. I'd bring out my polish rag and slipping it behind the shoe, I would pull it back and forth with both hands, rubbing it over the heel until it gleamed. Bringing it to the front, I'd stretch it across the toe of the shoe and again using two hands, pull up and down. When I was done, the shoe was buffed to a bright, clean shine.

I learned quickly that what made a shoeshine boy special was doing a perfect job as fast as he could. It also didn't hurt to have a little flair. I loved to pull my rags out quickly, popping them loudly in the air. I'd also pop the rag at the shoe with a flourish to show I was done. I charged ten cents a shine and often, I'd earn a tip. A good shine sometimes brought me a quarter.

Each day after school, I would run in the house and throw my books on my bed. I'd grab my box and head out. I had my favorite spots, stationing myself outside office buildings

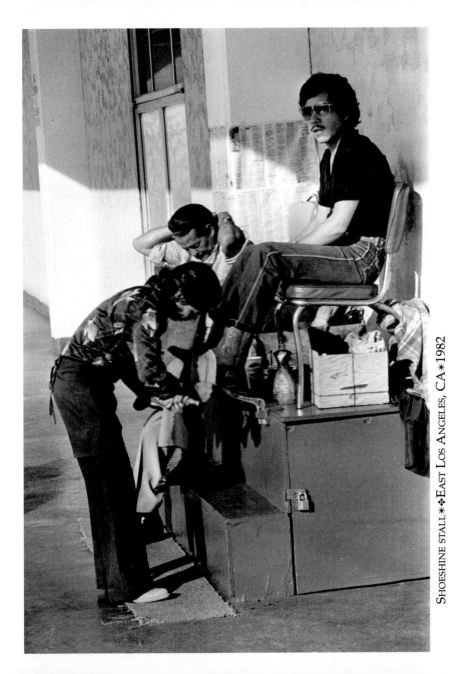

SHOESHINE STALL ❖ EAST LOS ANGELES, CA ✳ 1982

in time for the men going home.
Later, I'd head over to restaurants
and bars to catch the men as they
came and went after work.

Every night I came home in the
dark and my mother would be
waiting for me. I'd kiss her and she
would hold her hand out and I'd
put some money in it. ✳

NICOLÁS AT THE PANADERÍA＊DURHAM, NC＊2008

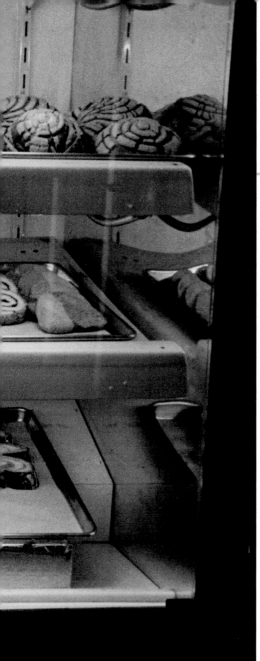

Ronquillo's Bakery

for my mother Lupe (1917-1987)

There was *pan de huevo* in four varieties. There were *pasteles* and *semitas* and *piedras*. Plump *empanadas* crowded close to each other in long lines. Apple and pumpkin and pineapple peeked out through cuts in their crust.

Next to them floated pink coconut rounds topped with fruit and nuts. Rectangles of *banderilla de Mexico* colored red, white, and green like the Mexican flag stood proudly at the end like soldiers.

Walking into the *panadería* was like walking into a warm, honey-colored dream. I wanted to try everything, especially the fluffy tiered cloud cakes that seemed big enough to feed my whole family but light enough to drift away.

My hands moved over the glass cases, my face close, looking at the trays upon trays of goodies. I had never seen so many cookies in one place. I wanted to eat them all. There were big round yellow ones and square ones and long, slender ones. There were the round snowballs of Mexican wedding cookies. Some had frosting. Others had rainbow sprinkles. Some were dusted with sugar and spices.

And then I saw the piggie. It was large and brown with a small snout and just the pinch of a tail. I could almost hear it oink.

"Do you want to see how we make *cochitos*?" asked Connie Ronquillo behind the counter.

These cookies and breads looked like fancy presents flown in from far-off places, fit for royalty. I couldn't believe that the Ronquillos had actually made them right there.

Mrs. Ronquillo pointed to a corner and I dropped my shoeshine box. I slipped through a small opening in the counter. She pushed open a swinging door and let me go in front of her.

Wearing a long white apron, Mr. Ronquillo was standing at a long table. In his hand was a large rolling pin almost as big as a baseball bat. He was pushing hard on the dough, stretching it out on the table, turning the pin and his body as he went first one way and then the other. The tendons in his forearms stood out with the effort.

I went to stand beside him. I could smell the spicy dough. It was a deep, rich brown and the sugar crystals in it glistened a little, like hidden jewels.

Then Mr. Ronquillo grabbed a cookie cutter in the shape of a pig and with two hands quickly cut out the cookies. The dough stuck to the cutter and he pulled it out with his fingers, dropping the piggies onto a long sheet.

He lifted the long tray above his head balancing it on his open hand. He opened the oven and the heat came at me like a gust of desert wind in summertime. With a flick of the wrist the tray slid into the oven. He must have done this a thousand times.

"You can't have one when they come out of there, they'll be too hot," he said wiping his floured hands on a cloth, "but you can have one from the front."

"Really?" I asked with big eyes. My breath caught. I had wanted a cookie so badly but wasn't sure the dime in my pocket was enough to buy one.

We went back up front and Mrs. Ronquillo handed me a *cochito* in wax paper. I took a bite. My tongue grew warm. I breathed out the cinnamon and ginger and felt the molasses dissolve. The dough stuck sweetly between my teeth. I had never eaten anything so good.

"I have a job for you, M'ijo." Mr. Ronquillo smiled down at me. "We always need boxes for big orders. If you find me the boxes, I'll give you a cookie for each one. Good, clean boxes. Is it a deal?"

I nodded over and over, thinking of all the cookies I would get. I knew my way around downtown and had seen plenty of boxes piled up in the alleyways. I'd be back in the bakery in a flash, picking out cookies and breads. In my mind, I planned to try each and every one of them.

"Deal," I replied.

BOY BALANCING BOXES∗LOS ANGELES, CA∗1982

Once a week, when I had finished shining shoes, I ran around collecting boxes. I'd stack them high in my arms and carry them carefully down the sidewalk to the bakery, dropping them in the back near the table. Then I'd stand for long minutes at the counter, choosing my cookies.

I'd take my prizes home to my mom who now had something sweet to go with her coffee every morning. My brothers fought over the chocolate-dipped. My little sister liked the ones with pink icing.

But as for me, my favorite was, and still is, the *cochito*. ∗

BOY COUNTING CHANGE✳TUCSON, AZ✳1994

Selling Papers

Somebody had come to the door. "Is your boy here?"
His voice was deep. "I want to see if he'd be interested in
something."

I could see the back of my mother's head moving as she
looked him up and down.

"M'ijo, there's a man here who wants to talk to you," she
yelled, never taking her eyes off of the man in front of her.

When I ventured out from where I had been watching, I
saw our neighbor Charlie Soto. He lived next door with his
mother and older sister but we'd never talked to him. He
was about 25 and he kept his hair in a perfect flat top.

Charlie rode a loud motorcycle that we could hear coming from far away. We would run outside to see it as he turned onto our block. It had handlebars that towered over him and a big back wheel that was larger than the front one.

Charlie also had a black Plymouth Fury with pointed tail fins - a shark on wheels. Like the motorcycle, it shined. Most Sunday afternoons we could see him washing and waxing them beneath his ramada.

"How'd you like to make some money?" he asked me as I stood next to my mother.

That was a silly question. When I wasn't in school, I spent most of my time making money. I shined shoes. I hustled soda bottles. I dug up torn comic books from the dump and sold them to other kids.

I was very curious. "What do you want me to do?"

"I manage all the paper boys and I was wondering if you'd like to sell newspapers after school for me," he said. "It won't cost you anything. You'll come by the loading dock and pick up the papers. When you're done selling, you'll come back to the loading dock and we'll settle up. Out of your earnings, we'll deduct what the papers cost. You'll make good money and keep all your tips."

I thought it over. Usually the hours right after school were slow ones for shining shoes. I reasoned that I could sell papers first and then once the restaurants and bars were filling up, I'd switch over to shining shoes.

"Where do I go and when do I start?" I asked.

"Let's go for a ride and I'll show you," he said.

"Can I, Mom?" Up until then the most exciting ride I had ever taken was hurtling down A Mountain on my bicycle with Bob perched on the handlebars. I'd never been on a motorcycle.

"Come right back," she yelled at me. I was already in his yard.

He swung his leg over and then held out a hand to me. I clambered up, not quite knowing where to put my feet. Behind me on the seat was a tall metal bar that I grasped with both hands.

The engine roared as he started it up. I lurched into his back as we went forward and then hung on tightly as we turned into the street.

Charlie took me first by my school. We went through the old barrio, past La Concha drugstore. I looked around hoping some of my friends were out and would see me.

We went over a few blocks to Stone Avenue. We headed north. Then we stopped right outside downtown in front of a three-story building. It was the newspaper building. He went slowly past the loading dock and pointed. Over his shoulder he said that the stacks of newspapers would be waiting there for me.

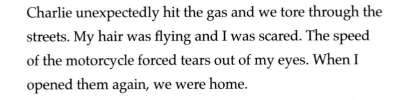

Charlie unexpectedly hit the gas and we tore through the
streets. My hair was flying and I was scared. The speed
of the motorcycle forced tears out of my eyes. When I
opened them again, we were home.

The next day, I ran home from school, grabbed my shoeshine box, and then headed to the newspaper building.
Charlie let me store my box in a corner of the office. Then
he handed me a stack.

I watched the other paperboys closely. Most of us were
young but there was a handful of old men who came
to get their stacks too. The old men had carts and they
would choose a spot in front of the larger office buildings
downtown and stand there.

The boys and I were more mobile. I carried the papers
under my arm and walked all over downtown,

MAN AND MOTORCYCLE*TUCSON, AZ*1999

approaching groups of people waiting at the bus stop. I held out the paper to passersby. Sometimes, if I was brave enough, I'd even enter the buildings and wander around. Whenever I came out, though, I couldn't meet the eye of the old man standing out front. I had undoubtedly robbed him of a sale.

It was very competitive and the stakes were high. For each paper I sold I made a couple of cents. Most days I would sell 20-30 copies. As in shining shoes, I relied on generous tippers.

When I had time, I would look through the newspapers I sold. It helped me to sell them. I'd yell out the headlines to anyone within earshot.

I quickly found out that reading the paper expanded my world. I knew much of inner Tucson like the back of my hand, but I'd never traveled very far from home. The newspaper had the latest scoop from around the whole city. I read about high school sports. I followed crime stories. I became interested in local and state politics. I looked closely at the photographs.

But there was much more than that in the paper. I began to read about places all over the world, most I'd never heard of. There was more happening out there than I could imagine.

Sundays were the best for selling newspapers. Charlie positioned his paperboys at busy intersections and outside churches. The Sunday papers were bigger, heavier, and more expensive, and I sold tons of them as people streamed out of church in their nicest clothes. On a good day, I could sell over a hundred papers. I could easily make more money on that one day than I could during the whole week.

Once the crowd was gone, I would head over first thing to El Charro restaurant to see Gilomeno, the cook. I go around back and pop my head in the open door. He not only bought a paper, but always made me a delicious burro for breakfast.

There couldn't have been a more perfect way to spend Sunday until the priest collared me. One day after Mass, he told me sternly that I was not allowed to sell papers unless I had attended church. After that, I sat in the last pew week after week, rushing up to get Communion before ducking out to set up at the bottom of the stairs.

BOYS AND MUSICIANS AT RESTAURANT*LOS ANGELES, CA*1982

A few years later, my brother Bob also got a job and on Sundays, he and I were in prime spots. I stood outside St. Augustine cathedral and Bob sold at the doors of All Saints a couple blocks away.

Once Bob got his job, we made a weekly ritual of going to a family dinner on Sunday afternoon. My mom was so proud as all of us walked down the street to El Minuto. I can only wonder what the owners thought as Bob and I scrounged around in our pockets and paid for the meals with crumbled dollar bills and all sorts of coins. ✶

SHINE BOY

BOY WITH PRESENT✳LOS ANGELES, CA✳1980

70

Christmas

Whenever I came home from shining shoes or selling papers, my mother always expected me to give her half of my earnings. I did this somewhat reluctantly and admittedly, I usually held back from the bargain most of the tips I'd earned. I felt those were extra and wholly mine.

As it was, my tips went to help out with household expenses anyway. Many times in the middle of the month when money grew tight, Mom would tell me to pick up some groceries before coming home. Or I would buy things for the home that made all our lives better. When I was a teenager, for instance, I brought home a second TV for the room I shared with my brothers so we could watch different programs than those my mother insisted we watch on her set. She loved Lawrence Welk. We didn't.

So when Christmastime came around, I was able to pay for my own gifts for the family. December in Tucson brought mild and sunny weather during the day. But as we headed off to school, the mornings were dry and cold. Our breath drifted in the air like smoke.

I'd been saving my tips since Thanksgiving. I was tempted a few times to spend some of it on candy, but I had my heart set on buying Christmas presents.

After I had counted out a few dollars for my mom's tamale supplies, I ventured out into downtown. Someone had sparkled up the street with stars hanging between the light posts. The stores held idyllic scenes in their front windows. I had only seen real snow once before and it didn't last long but by pressing my nose to the glass, I would peer at the fake snow that littered the display and wonder at how cold it was.

I had a plan in mind, gifts that I thought each one would like. Chem was always hogging the radio and singing along. I'd get him some records. Bob was easy to buy for. He and I liked the same things so whatever struck me as fun would be good for him. Sylvia needed a new doll.

My mom was always careful about her appearance. She really knew how to dress and she always made herself up before heading to the dances on Saturday nights. My dad, on the other hand, couldn't get enough handkerchiefs or work clothes.

I stopped in front of the Kress building, the fanciest department store on Congress Street. I couldn't afford the things inside but I liked visiting their toy department to finger the newest stuff. Every afternoon of the week before, I had gone in and out of the store to see Santa. I stood in line over and over and over, and each time I sat on Santa's lap, I came up with a new wish list. Afterwards, Santa handed me a candy cane. I had gone so many times, we were able to decorate the tree with all the canes I'd been given.

My favorite display was in the basement of the Sears store. It was a giant toy train that ran through a town complete with trees, bridges, buildings, cows and horses. All month I had snuck in there, when I was supposed to be selling papers, to watch that train go around.

After I'd checked out all the Christmas displays, I headed into Woolworths. They had records three for a dollar. The teenage girl who worked there helped me make a selection for Chem. Then I bought toys for Bob and Sylvia.

The drugstore seemed like a good place to find a gift for Mom. I had never shopped for ladies' stuff before. I wandered among the lipsticks, hair products and perfumes.

There was a lady behind the counter watching me. "Do you want to smell one?" she asked. "We have sample bottles you can try."

She laughed when I answered, "I'm not spraying that stuff. I don't want to smell girly!"

She took the bottle and sprayed it in the air. I sniffed. It seemed good. I bought the smallest bottle.

I knew exactly where to head for my dad: the hardware store. I loved it in there. They had camping equipment, fishing poles, basketball hoops, hammers, and work clothes. I looked around and wondered if I'd ever grow large enough to use any of this stuff.

The salesman asked me, "What size is your dad, little man?"

"He's big," I said, shrugging my shoulders.

BOY DRESSED AS SANTA∗LOS ANGELES, CA∗1981

"Hmm, big," he said. He went over to a rack of shirts and chose one. "This should fit him. You want me to wrap it for you?"

I hurried home with all the presents. Everyone was watching TV in the front room. I went around to the back, quickly wrapped the other presents in newspaper and stuck them under my bed. Later I snuck out and placed them under the tree.

I loved watching their faces as they opened the gifts I had chosen. My favorite present that year was the big plate of tamales with rice and beans that Mom fixed just for me. ✳

BARBERS✳TUCSON, AZ✳2002

Barber Shop

I followed my usual route around downtown looking for shoes to shine. Box in hand, I descended into the Stone Avenue underpass away from downtown toward a park on Speedway Boulevard.

The route took me past Padias' Barber Shop many times. On Saturdays especially the barber shop was busy. Shaggy men filed in for a haircut and a shave. They came out all cleaned up and ready for their Saturday night dates.

As I lingered on the sidewalk hoping to snag another customer, I heard someone call to me. Rudy Padias stood in the doorway, dressed in a white barber's shirt and pressed pants. He was a good advertisement for his shop. He had short, trimmed hair parted in the middle with a small mustache.

"I have some shoes that need fixing up. You think you can do it?"

"I can do anything," I told him.

I had never been inside the shop. I got my hair cut downtown at the barbers' college. Our school principal, Mrs. Lawrence would take a group of us over there whenever our hair got unruly.

On one side of Padias' shop was a row of chairs where the men sat to wait their turn. A table stacked with magazines and newspapers gave them something to do. Facing the chairs were two barber seats, one for Rudy and the other for his partner, Ed. Behind them was a wall-length mirror.

Rudy came back from the rear room with a big pair of shoes. He turned them over just once before he handed them to me. They had sharp, pointed spikes on their soles.

I had never seen anything like them before. I held the heavy shoes together in one hand, turned them over, and looked again at the spikes.

"They're golf shoes." Rudy smiled at me.

The closest I'd gotten to golf was my cousin Güero who worked as a caddy during the summer and on weekends at El Rio golf course next to Barrio Hollywood. Not much later, I'd see the name of pro golfer Lee Trevino, the Merry Mexican, on the sports page.

The spikes were filled with dry red clay. Bits of grass stuck out here and there. I knelt down and got to work. I cleaned them with my stiff brush foaming with saddle soap. I had to apply the polish carefully because the shoes were black and white. Soon they were gleaming.

Rudy left the man he was shaving to return to me. He fished out a couple of quarters out of his pocket to pay me.

"I've been looking for someone to help out around here. I want you to come in on Saturdays and shine the shoes of the customers. You'll make some good tips. Then I want you to sweep the floor after I'm done."

He would clean up their heads and faces, and I would shine up their shoes. With the right clothes, the men would look spiffy from head to toe.

I quickly thought it over. The men in the shop would be guaranteed customers and on top of that, they'd be stuck in their seats. They might wave me off like some men did on the street but at least I wouldn't have to run them down.

He wiped his hand on his smock and held it out to me. We shook on our agreement.

On Saturdays, I would spend all afternoon in the barber shop. It had a big window that looked toward downtown. When I wasn't busy, I would sit on a stool and watch the trains go over the underpass. I'd count the number of boxcars and wonder what was inside and where they were going.

MAN IN MARKET*LOS ANGELES, CA*1987

Other times, I would watch Ed working with his polished rocks. He fashioned them into bolo ties, money clips, and other objects. I loved seeing a plain rock become a shiny gem.

Sometimes Rudy would ask me if I was hungry. I usually was.

"Go next door and get us a couple of ham sandwiches. Tell Sam they're for Rudy."

It was cool and dark inside the Tally Ho. Along one side was a high bar where men I recognized from the produce warehouses were eating and drinking. They would buy

newspapers from me in the afternoons and toss me a piece of fruit to munch on. On the other side of the restaurant were the family tables covered with pizzas, salads, and big baskets of garlic bread.

I placed the order with Sam, the large man behind the swinging door that led to the kitchen. I watched as he stirred big pots of bubbling water and ladled tomato sauce onto the top of almost every dish. Soon he found time to assemble our sandwiches: piles of thin ham on long crusty bread.

When the barber shop would close, I would wave goodbye to Ed and Rudy and head back into the Tally Ho to shine the shoes of the men at the bar and get some pizza. ✳

Entering the Newsroom

Durazo's Service Station was located behind the newspaper building on Stone Avenue north of downtown. Buster Durazo fixed flats, changed oil, and ran two parking lots.

It was a small station. On one side of the building was a covered bay with a lift. On the other side was an open area where he would hire me to wash cars.

Inside, the back wall was lined with various hoses, tires, and batteries. There was a desk with a cash register. Buster's sister Olivia sat there in the daytime. Behind her was the coldest soda machine in the area. This was what drew me there in the first place.

Buster had a ton of friends. In the evenings, when I would come by, there was always someone sitting in the one chair reserved for customers.

I used to put down my shoeshine box, nurse my soda, and listen to the men tell each other the news. They were always talking about City Hall or how business was going. Occasionally a customer would ask for a shine.

One of Buster's largest customers was the newspaper itself. He serviced their fleet, making sure the trucks were in good repair and gassed up. I loved to help him pump the gasoline and clean the windshields.

One evening the phone rang. "Yep, he's here," Buster said. "I'll send him up."

When he hung up the phone, he told me that Helen Hitchcock, the Star's switchboard operator, who had a talent for knowing just where to find people, was calling to see if I'd come up to the newsroom. One of the sports reporters wanted a shine.

I knew the loading dock out back well enough, of course, where I picked up my stack of papers, but I'd never been inside the building. Buster instructed me. "Take the front door and go up to the third floor. Someone there will direct you."

Out front of the building, little balconies hung over the sidewalk and tall palo verde trees grew out of concrete containers. There were three different sets of doors to enter. The first two doors were locked, but the third opened.

It was late and the building was quiet. My sneakers slapped on the steps as I trudged up the stairs, box in hand. There was a door at the top that read "Arizona Daily Star" in the same script as the masthead of the paper.

I opened the door and before me was a big desk. The receptionist had gone home already. When I looked around some more, I saw a glass-enclosed office on my left. A man with wavy, gray hair sat at a typewriter. I pushed the swinging wooden door and nervously poked my head into his office.

"Can I help you?" he asked as he peered up from his half glasses. Around him were lots of papers. There were plaques on the wall.

"I'm looking for the sports department. A man wants a shoeshine there," I said.

He sized me up. I don't know what he thought of me. I'm sure I was a little wide-eyed. I had never been in a fancy office before. He stood up and placed his hand on my shoulder, turning me around. "I'll show you. My name is Vic Thornton. What's yours?"

We walked past desks occupied my men and women on telephones. Some were pecking away at typewriters. The room was alive. Everywhere there was activity. In one section a bunch of older men were reading pages of paper and scribbling on them. At another desk a man was being interviewed by a reporter.

Until that point I had never thought of how a newspaper was made. As I looked around, I realized that these were the people who wrote the stories that filled its pages. They knew important people. They traveled. They asked questions and they told us the answers. Every single day they put it all together and created a neatly-folded paper with lots of sections that I then sold on the street.

The newsroom was almost like a maze. We turned this way and that following a path that I couldn't quite make out. At one corner, we walked past a noisy room where funny little machines ran their fingers back and forth and spat out pages and pages of type. What I

TEEN WRAPPED IN FLAG✳WINSTON SALEM, NC✳2006

learned later was that these were the wire machines, receiving stories from all over the world.

At last we reached our destination. Mr. Thornton handed me off to Ed Gallardo. He was Mexican American like me. He was dressed in a sports shirt and had the casual attitude of an athlete.

The experience changed me forever. I knew without a doubt that I wanted to work in that newsroom someday. And after that first night, they couldn't get rid of me. I returned to the newsroom, night after night. I shined the shoes of the reporters heading out for interviews. I ran errands for them for dimes. I carried their camera bags. I sat at their desks as they worked and tried to learn all I could. I never wanted to leave.

Later, Vic put me on the payroll as a copy boy. I answered phones, filled glue pots, sharpened pencils, and ripped stories off the teletype machines. I worked there as I made my way through college and when I graduated, they made me a staff photographer.

Years earlier, when my father made me that shoeshine box, he and I both knew that it would open up a world of independence. If only he could have seen where it led me. ✴

TEENAGERS COMING FROM SCHOOL∗TUCSON, AZ∗1976

About José

José Galvez was born in Tucson. Arizona. He is a graduate of the UA School of Journalism. He was a staff photographer for the *Arizona Daily Star* and the *Los Angeles Times*. In 1984, he served on an *LA Times* team that won a Pulitzer Prize for a series on Latino life in Southern California. Since leaving the newspaper business, Galvez has helped mount national exhibitions of Latino art. He has published various books and has been awarded grants and commissions. He has exhibited his photographs in museums and galleries nationwide and abroad. He also takes his work to events where people can see the work for free: libraries and public schools, colleges and universities, as well as fiestas, rodeos, and lowrider shows.

A nationally-known speaker and artist, Galvez continues his mission of documenting Hispanic communities across the United States. Learn more at www.josegalvez.com.